TODAY'S HITS
Playalong *for* Clarinet

Don't Stop Movin' 10
S Club 7

Eternal Flame 6
Atomic Kitten

Let Love Be Your Energy 8
Robbie Williams

Only For A While 16
Toploader

Out Of Reach 13
Gabrielle

Pure And Simple 27
Hear'Say

Run For Cover 18
Sugababes

Sail Away 20
David Gray

Sing 24
Travis

What Took You So Long? 30
Emma Bunton

Clarinet Fingering Chart 3

This publication is not authorised for sale in the
United States of America and/or Canada

WISE PUBLICATIONS
London/New York/Paris/Sydney/Copenhagen/Madrid/Tokyo

Exclusive Distributors:
Music Sales Limited
8/9 Frith Street, London W1D 3JB, England.
Music Sales Pty Limited
120 Rothschild Avenue, Rosebery, NSW 2018, Australia.

Order No. AM966020
ISBN 0-7119-8362-3
This book © Copyright 2001 by Wise Publications.

Unauthorised reproduction of any part of this publication by
any means including photocopying is an infringement of copyright.

Compiled by Nick Crispin.
Music arranged by Simon Lesley.
Music processed by Enigma Music Production Services.
Cover photography by George Taylor.
Printed in the United Kingdom by Page Bros., Norwich, Norfolk.

CD produced by Jonas Perrson.
Instrumental solos by John Whelan.
All guitars by Arthur Dick.
Engineered by Kester Sims.

Your Guarantee of Quality:
As publishers, we strive to produce every book to
the highest commercial standards.
The music has been freshly engraved and the book has been
carefully designed to minimise awkward page turns and
to make playing from it a real pleasure.
Particular care has been given to specifying acid-free, neutral-sized
paper made from pulps which have not been elemental chlorine bleached.
This pulp is from farmed sustainable forests and was
produced with special regard for the environment.
Throughout, the printing and binding have been planned to
ensure a sturdy, attractive publication which should give years of enjoyment.
If your copy fails to meet our high standards,
please inform us and we will gladly replace it.

Music Sales' complete catalogue describes thousands of
titles and is available in full colour sections by subject,
direct from Music Sales Limited.
Please state your areas of interest and send a
cheque/postal order for £1.50 for postage to:
Music Sales Limited, Newmarket Road, Bury St. Edmunds, Suffolk IP33 3YB.

www.musicsales.com

Clarinet Fingering Chart

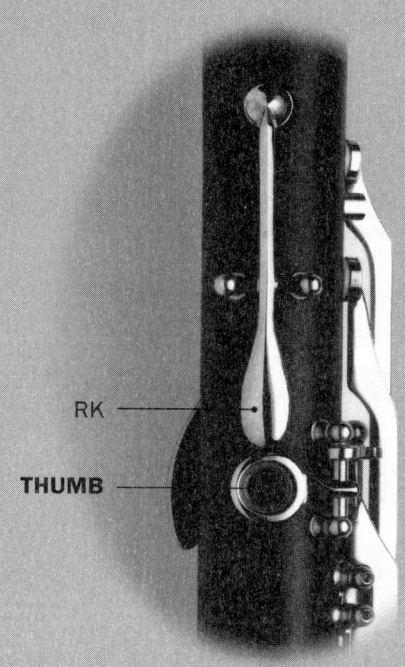

RK
THUMB

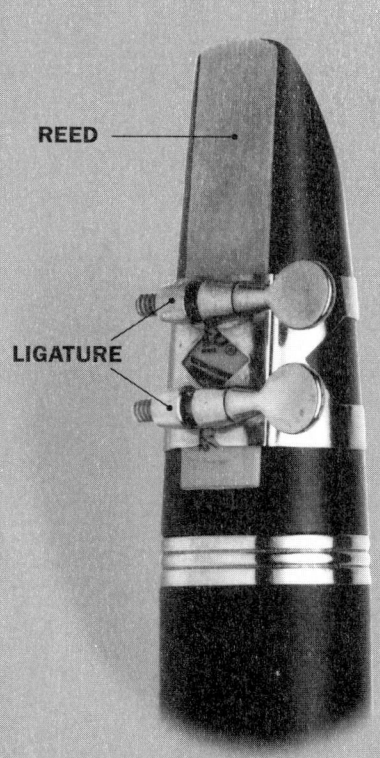

REED
LIGATURE

Mouthpiece

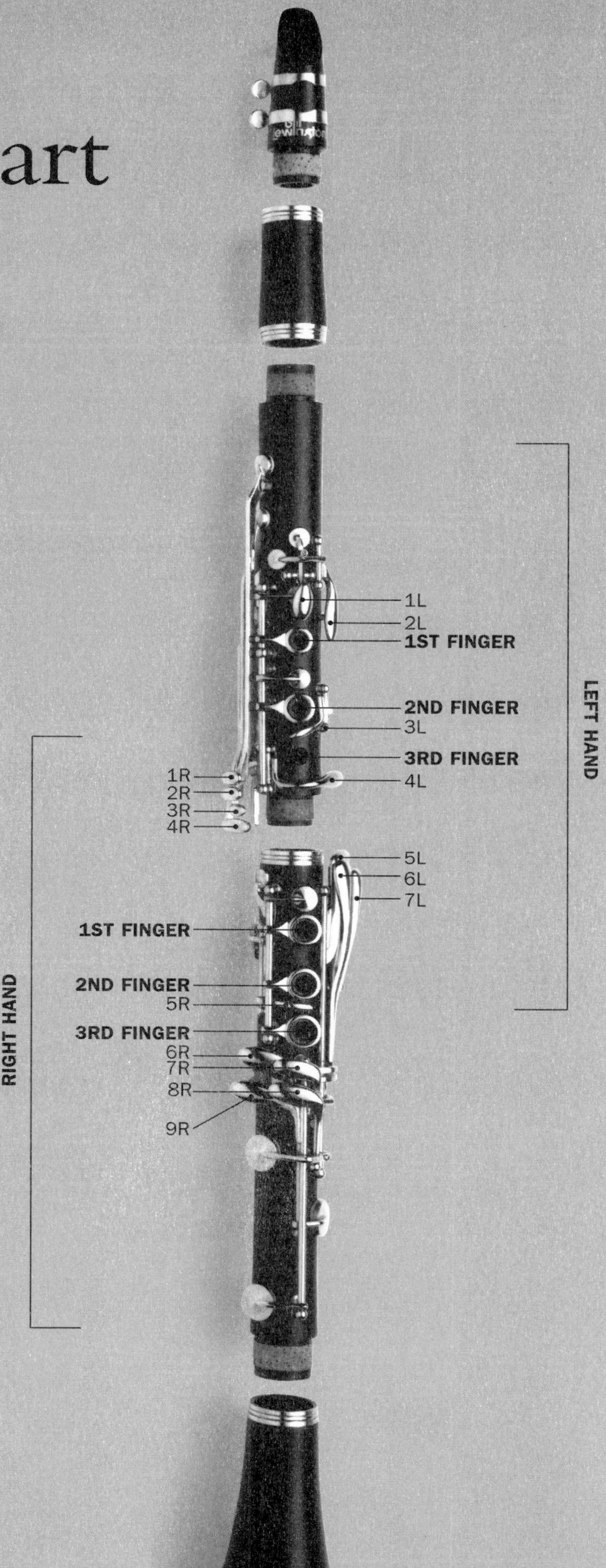

1L
2L
1ST FINGER

2ND FINGER
3L
3RD FINGER
1R
2R
4L
3R
4R

5L
6L
7L
1ST FINGER

2ND FINGER
5R
3RD FINGER
6R
7R
8R
9R

LEFT HAND

RIGHT HAND

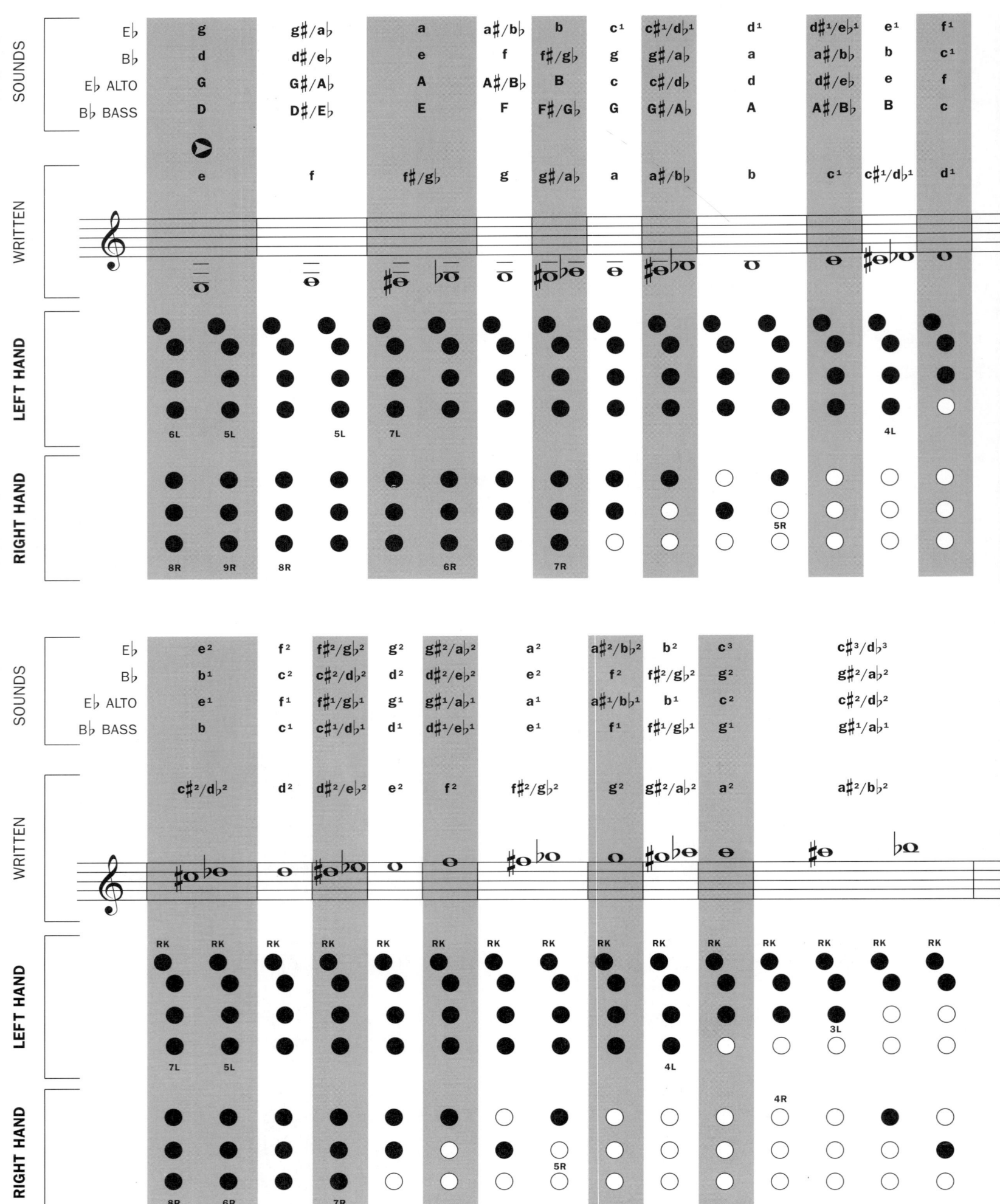

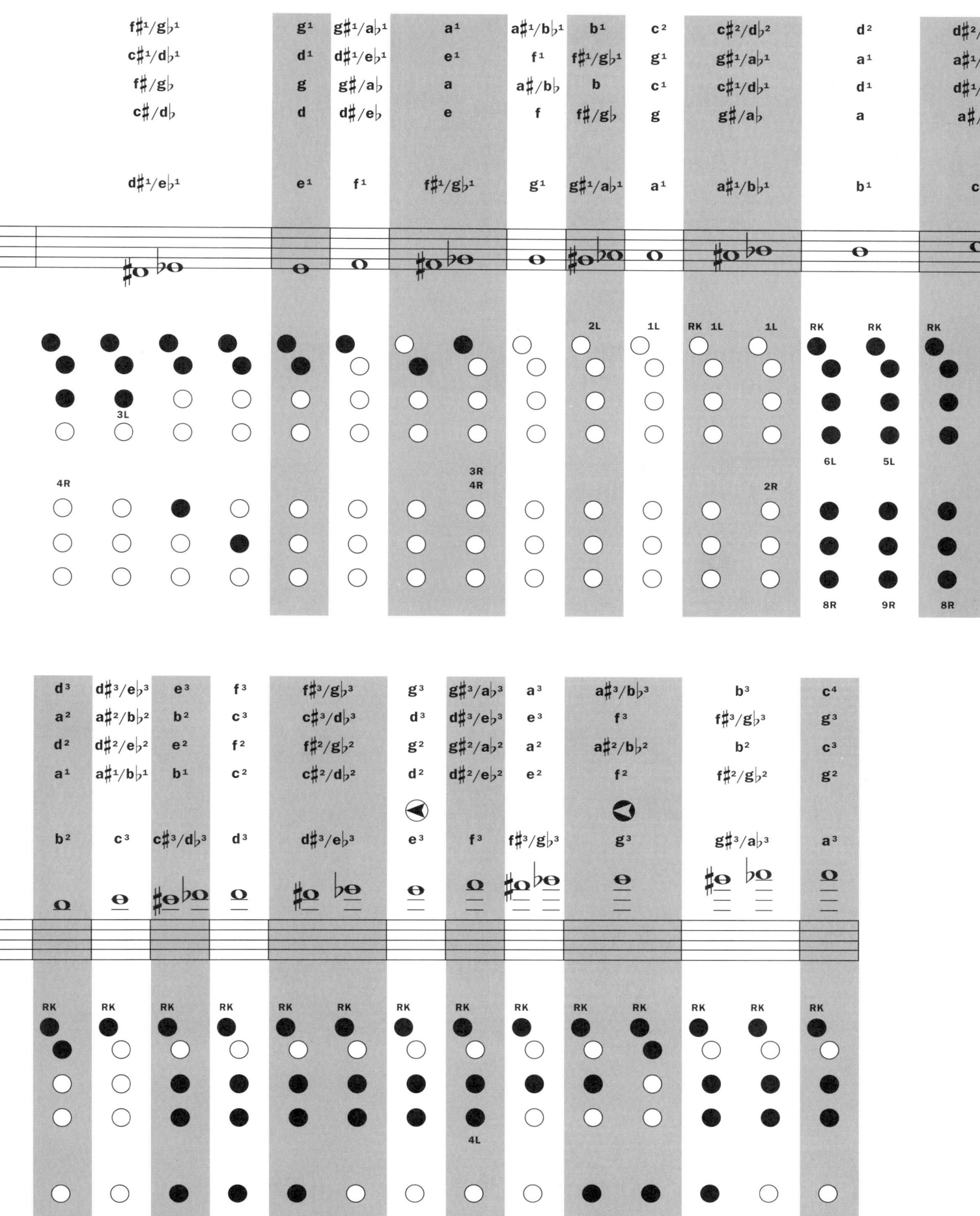

Eternal Flame

Words & Music by Billy Steinberg, Tom Kelly & Susanna Hoffs

© Copyright 1988 & 1989 Billy Steinberg Music/Sony/ATV Tunes LLC/Bangophile Music, USA.
Sony/ATV Music Publishing (UK) Limited, 10 Great Marlborough Street, London W1F 7LP (66.66%)/
Universal Music Publishing Limited, Elsinore House, 77 Fulham Palace Road, London W6 8JA (33.34%).
All Rights Reserved. International Copyright Secured.

Let Love Be Your Energy

Words & Music by Robbie Williams & Guy Chambers

Don't Stop Movin'

Words & Music by Simon Ellis, Sheppard Solomon & S Club 7

© Copyright 2001 19 Music Limited/BMG Music Publishing Limited,
Bedford House, 69-79 Fulham High Street, London SW6 3JW (37.5%)/
Rondor Music (London) Limited, 10a Parsons Green, London SW6 4TW (37.5%)/
Universal Music Publishing Limited, Elsinore House, 77 Fulham Palace Road, London W6 8JA (25%).
All Rights Reserved. International Copyright Secured.

25
28
32
f
36
40
3
46
mp
50
ff legato

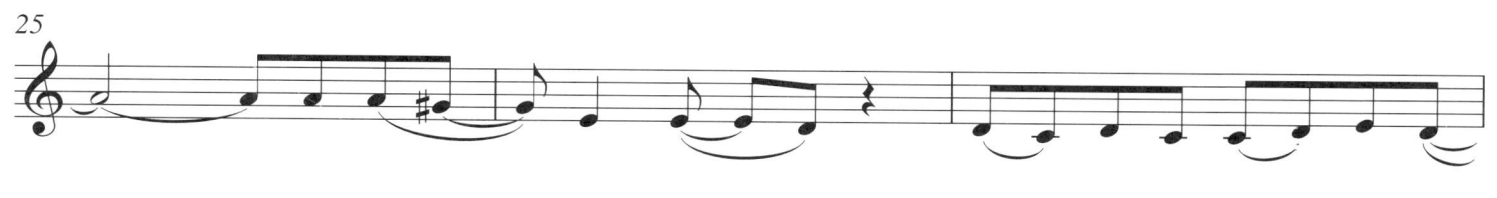

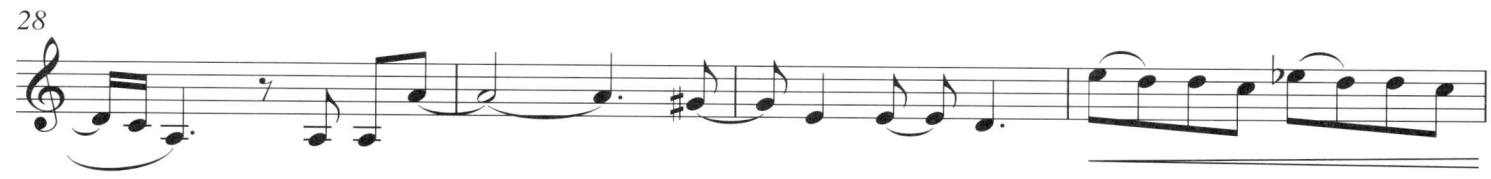

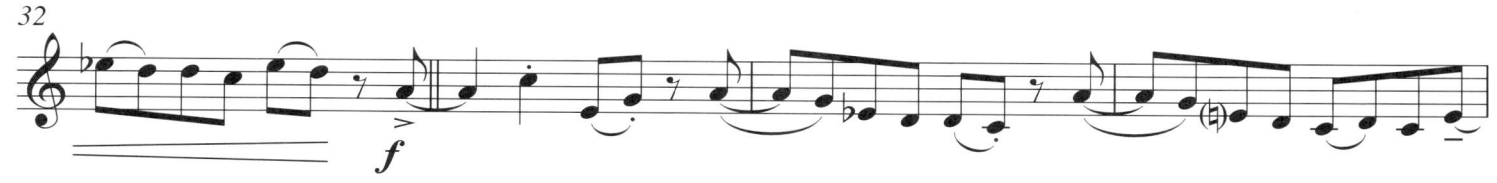

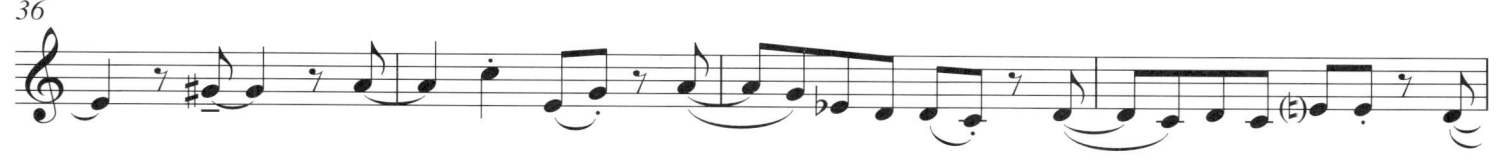

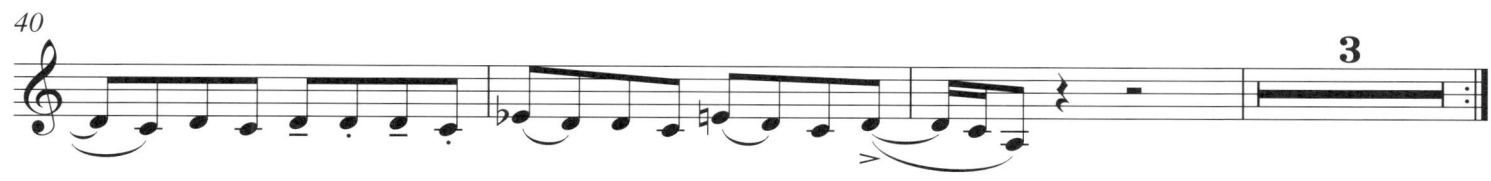

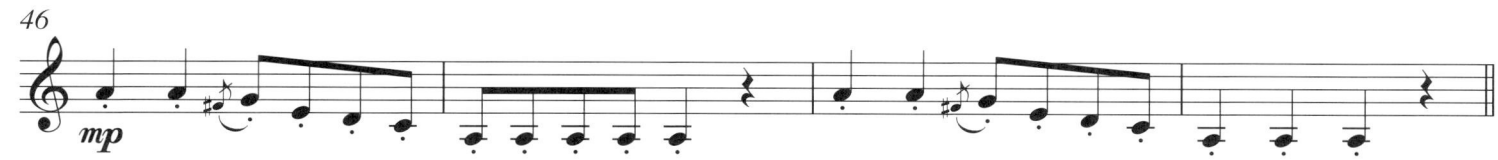

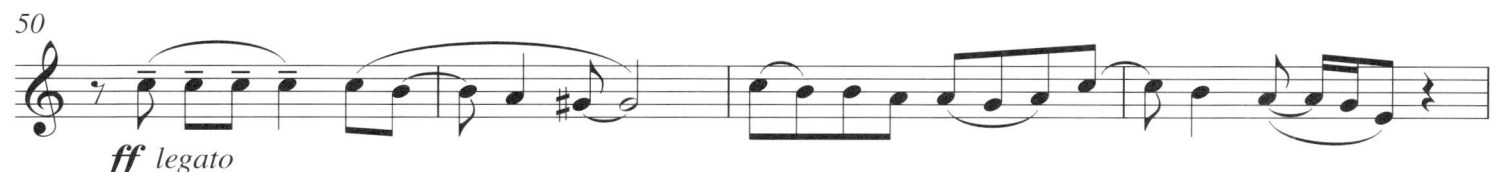

Out Of Reach

Words & Music by Gabrielle & Jonathan Shorten

Only For A While

Words & Music by Joseph Washbourn

© Copyright 1999 Universal Music Publishing Limited, 77 Fulham Palace Road, London W6 8JA.
All Rights Reserved. International Copyright Secured.

Step into the spotlight with...
GUEST SPOT
...and playalong *with* the specially recorded backing tracks

A great book and CD series,
each title available in arrangements for
**FLUTE, CLARINET, ALTO SAXOPHONE,
TENOR SAXOPHONE*, TRUMPET* and VIOLIN***

Pull Out

Now you can own professional

when you play all these

for Clarinet, Flute, Alto Saxophone

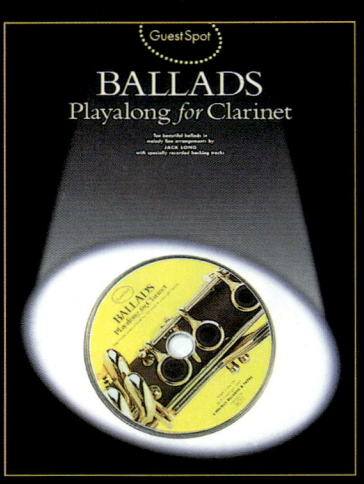
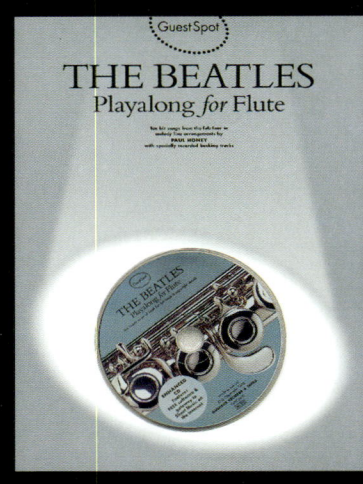
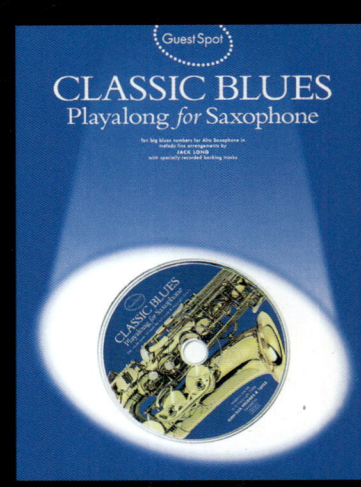

The *essential* book & CD series...

From Jazz, Blues and Swing to Ballads, Showstoppers, Film and TV Themes, here are all your favourite Chart Hits and more! *Check out* the special editions featuring legends of pop, **Abba** and **The Beatles**.

The Music Book...

Top line arrangements for 10 songs, *plus* a fingering guide for wind instruments.

The CD...

Hear full performance versions of all the songs. Then play along with the recorded accompaniments.

ABBA
Includes:
Dancing Queen
Fernando
Mamma Mia
Waterloo
AM960905 Clarinet
AM960894 Flute
AM960916 Alto Saxophone
AM960927 Violin

BALLADS
Includes:
Candle In The Wind
Imagine
Killing Me Softly With His Song
Wonderful Tonight
AM941787 Clarinet
AM941798 Flute
AM941809 Alto Saxophone

THE BEATLES
Includes:
All You Need Is Love
Hey Jude
Lady Madonna
Yesterday
NO90682 Clarinet
NO90683 Flute
NO90684 Alto Saxophone

CHRISTMAS
Includes:
Frosty The Snowman
Have Yourself A Merry Little Christmas
Mary's Boy Child
Winter Wonderland
AM950400 Clarinet
AM950411 Flute
AM950422 Alto Saxophone

have your very backing band...

great melody line arrangements
Tenor Saxophone*, Trumpet* and Violin*

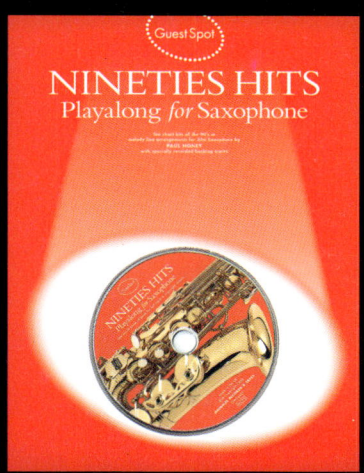

CLASSIC BLUES
Includes:
Fever
Harlem Nocturne
Moonglow
Round Midnight

AM941743 Clarinet
AM941754 Flute
AM941765 Alto Saxophone

CLASSICS
Includes:
Air On The 'G' String - Bach
Jupiter (from The Planets Suite) - Holst
Ode To Joy (Theme from Symphony No.9 'Choral') - Beethoven
Swan Lake (Theme) - Tchaikovsky.

AM955537 Clarinet
AM955548 Flute
AM955560 Violin

FILM THEMES
Includes:
Circle Of Life (The Lion King)
Love Is All Around (Four Weddings & A Funeral)
Moon River (Breakfast At Tiffany's)
You Must Love Me (Evita)

AM941864 Clarinet
AM941875 Flute
AM941886 Alto Saxophone

JAZZ
Includes:
Fly Me To The Moon
Opus One
Satin Doll
Straight No Chaser

AM941700 Clarinet
AM941710 Flute
AM941721 Alto Saxophone

NINETIES HITS
Includes:
Falling Into You (Celine Dion)
Never Ever (All Saints)
Tears In Heaven (Eric Clapton)
2 Become 1 (Spice Girls)

AM952853 Clarinet
AM952864 Flute
AM952875 Alto Saxophone

No.1 HITS
Includes:
A Whiter Shade Of Pale (Procol Harum)
Every Breath You Take (The Police)
No Matter What (Boyzone)
Unchained Melody (The Righteous Brothers).

AM955603 Clarinet
AM955614 Flute
AM955625 Alto Saxophone
AM959530 Violin

SHOWSTOPPERS
Includes:
Big Spender (Sweet Charity)
Bring Him Home (Les Misérables)
I Know Him So Well (Chess)
Somewhere (West Side Story)

AM941820 Clarinet
AM941831 Flute
AM941842 Alto Saxophone

SWING
Includes:
I'm Getting Sentimental Over You
Is You Is Or Is You Ain't My Baby?
Perdido
Tuxedo Junction

AM949377 Clarinet
AM960575 Trumpet
AM949399 Alto Saxophone
AM959618 Tenor Saxophone

TV THEMES
Includes:
Black Adder
Home And Away
London's Burning
Star Trek

AM941908 Clarinet
AM941919 Flute
AM941920 Alto Saxophone

* Selected titles only

Sample the *whole* series of *Guest Spot* with these special double CD bumper compilations...

GUEST SPOT GOLD
Twenty all-time Hit Songs, Showstoppers and Film Themes

Includes:
A Whiter Shade Of Pale (Procol Harum)
Bridge Over Troubled Water
  (Simon & Garfunkel)
Don't Cry For Me Argentina (from Evita)
Yesterday (The Beatles)
Where Do I Begin (Theme from Love Story)
Words (Boyzone)
Yesterday (The Beatles)

AM960729 Clarinet
AM960718 Flute
AM960730 Alto Saxophone

GUEST SPOT PLATINUM
Seventeen greatest Chart Hits, Ballads and Film Themes

Includes:
Circle Of Life (from The Lion King)
Candle In The Wind (Elton John)
Dancing Queen (Abba)
Falling Into You (Celine Dion)
I Believe I Can Fly (R. Kelly)
Take My Breath Away (Berlin)
Torn (Natalie Imbruglia)

AM960751 Clarinet
AM960740 Flute
AM960762 Alto Saxophone

Available from all good music retailers or,
in case of difficulty, contact:

Music Sales Limited
Newmarket Road, Bury St. Edmunds, Suffolk IP33 3YB.
Telephone 01284 725725   Fax 01284 702592

www.musicsales.com

Run For Cover

Words & Music by Cameron McVey, Johnny Lipsey, Paul Simm, Siobhan Donaghy, Keisha Buchanan & Mutya Buena

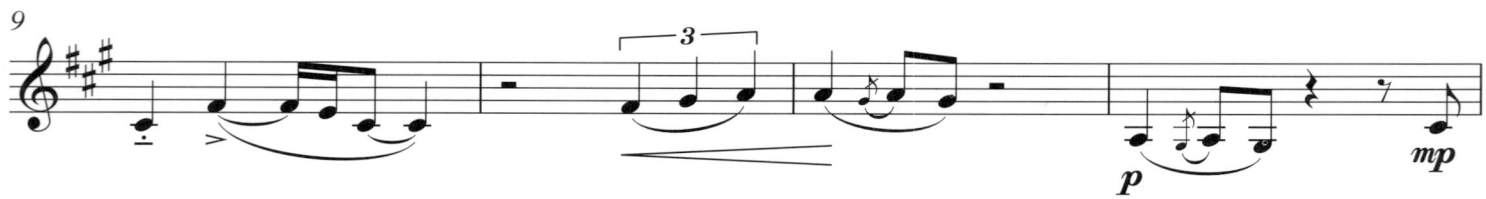

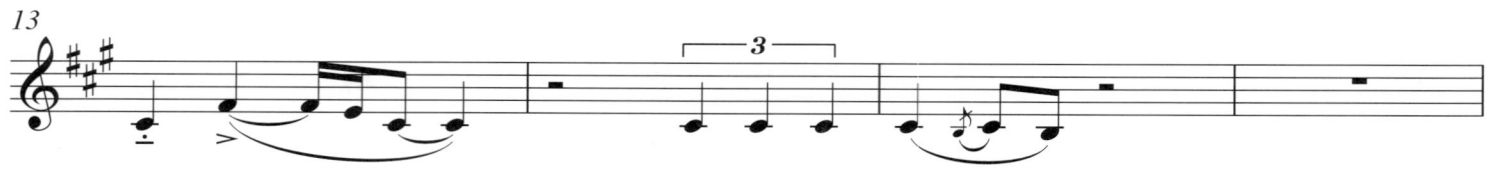

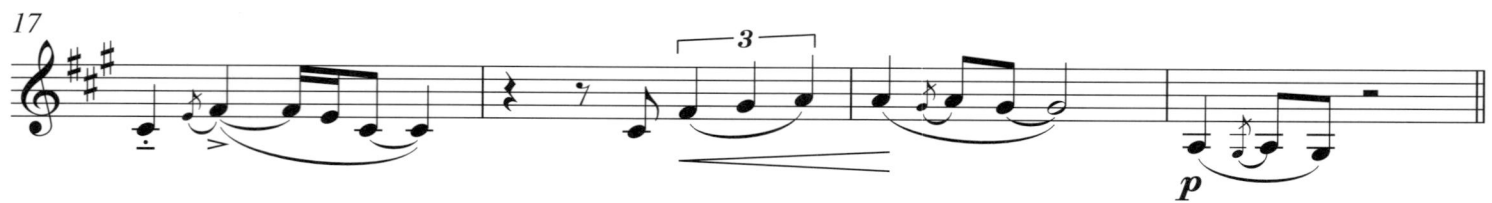

© Copyright 2000 EMI Music Publishing Limited, 127 Charing Cross Road, London WC2 0EA (45%)/
Sony/ATV Music Publishing (UK) Limited, 10 Great Marlborough Street, London W1F 7LP (25%)/
Copyright Control (30%).
All Rights Reserved. International Copyright Secured.

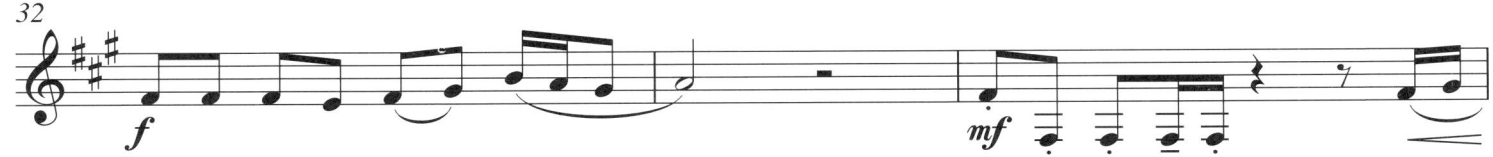
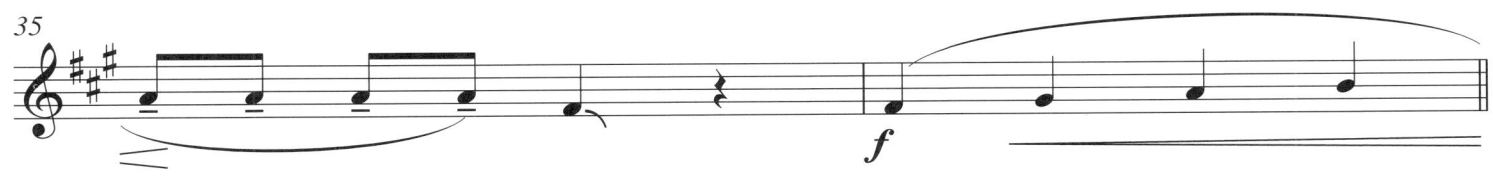

Sail Away

Words & Music by David Gray

Sing

Words & Music by Fran Healy

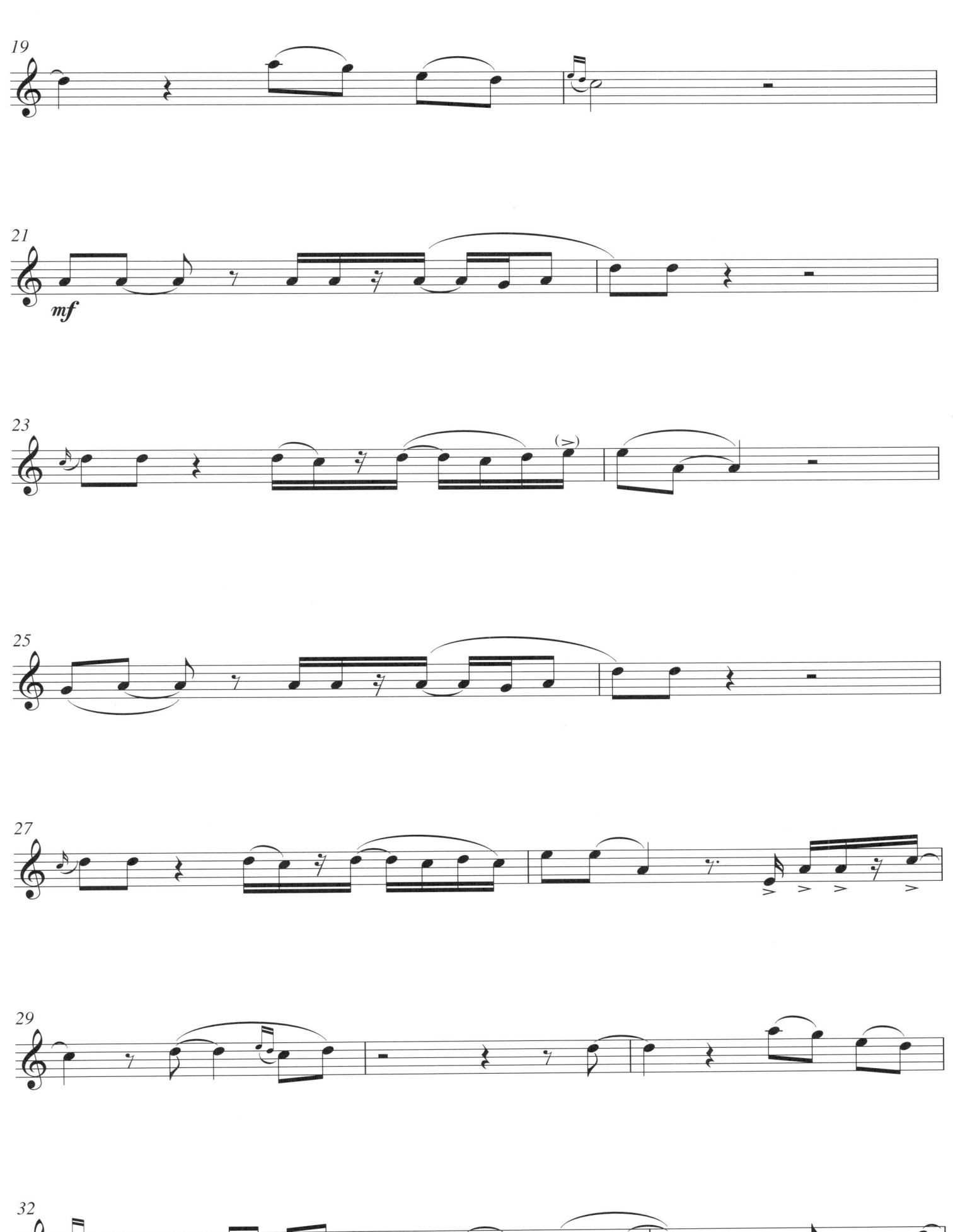

Pure And Simple

Words & Music by Tim Hawes, Pete Kirtley & Alison Clarkson

What Took You So Long?

Words & Music by Emma Bunton, Richard Stannard, Julian Gallagher, Martin Harrington, John Themis & Dave Morgan

© Copyright 2001 EMI Music Publishing (WP) Limited, 127 Charing Cross Road, London WC2 0EA (48.5%)/
Sony/ATV Music Publishing (UK) Limited, 10 Great Marlborough Street, London W1F 7LP (23.5%)/
Biffco Music Publishing Limited/Universal Music Publishing Limited, Elsinore House, 77 Fulham Palace Road, London W6 8JA (15%)/
Chrysalis Music Limited, The Chrysalis Building, Bramley Road, London W10 6SP (13%).
All Rights Reserved. International Copyright Secured.

Herbert Howells

Organ Sonata No.1 in C minor

edited by
Graham Matthews and Robin Wells

Order No: NOV010229

NOVELLO PUBLISHING LIMITED

NOTE

In *Memories of Choirs and Cloisters* (London, 1931) Sir Herbert Brewer (1865 – 1928) remembered the 'serious-minded' Herbert Howells as one of his pupils, contrasting Howells with the 'light-hearted' Ivor Davies, later known as Ivor Novello.

Howells (1892 – 1983), born in Lydney, Gloucestershire, studied with Brewer from 1905, being articled to the distinguished Cathedral organist and composer in 1909. Eric Blom, in Grove 5, writes of Howells that 'in the summer of 1911 he withdrew from Gloucester Cathedral in order to devote himself to composition, and . . . the works he composed gained him, in February 1912, an open scholarship at the RCM (Royal College of Music) in London' where he studied composition with Stanford, and harmony and counterpoint with Charles Wood. One of these early compositions was the Organ Sonata in C Minor, dedicated to Ambrose Porter and listed in Grove 5 as being Opus 1 from 1911.

From 1900 to 1913 Porter was with Brewer at Gloucester Cathedral, being assistant organist from 1907. Porter dedicated a Fugue in C minor to his friend Herbert Howells; and he kept his friendship in good repair. In 1925 Porter was appointed cathedral organist at Lichfield, a post he retained until 1959. During his time at Lichfield he played the Howells Sonata from the original manuscript which was in his possession. This manuscript is believed to have been destroyed after his death. Barry Draycott, a pupil of Porter, and Richard Lloyd, both of whom heard the sonata played by Porter, have verified independently that the work published here and as recorded by Graham Matthews is in fact the very piece they knew at Lichfield.

Tustin Baker, another pupil of Brewer, also came to know this early Howells organ work. Always an admirer of Howells' music, he copied out by hand the early C Minor Sonata, and had it well bound with gold-blocked titling. The work was described as the composer's Opus 2. As with Porter, Dr Baker was a long-serving cathedral organist: he was then at Sheffield Cathedral. After his sudden death in 1966, Mrs Baker passed the copy to Hubert Stafford, sub-organist at Sheffield Cathedral at the time. Following the appointment of Graham Matthews to the Cathedral as Master of the Music in 1967, Hubert Stafford passed on to him the copy for safe-keeping.

There is evidence in the manuscript copy that Tustin Baker worked on the slow movement, possibly recognizing its closeness in atmosphere and style to Howells' Psalm-Prelude Set 1, No. 2. But it is evident from the many errors of transcription (mostly accidentals), that it would have been impossible to play the first movement in its copied state, further marred by the unaccountable lacuna of two completely blank bars in the exposition (bars 45 and 46).

We have corrected the errors and inconsistencies; and Graham Matthews has adapted some of the original indications of registration for a four-manual instrument to enable performance on a three-manual instrument. Bars 214-15 in the first movement recapitulation have been reworked to supply material for the two blank bars in the exposition. The editorial practice has been strongly influenced by the need to produce a performing edition, unencumbered by apparatus of the kind that hinders ready learning and appreciation. Directions within square brackets and slurs with a vertical slash are editorial.

When Howells withdrew from Gloucester Cathedral in 1911 he was, in Eric Blom's account, 'at that time entirely self-taught as regards the creative side of his art'. What must surely have made the Sonata a recognizably significant precursor of so much finely-wrought music to be written throughout the composer's lifetime was the disciplined approach to Sonata Form in the first movement, the controlled lyricism of the second, and the mastery of fugal writing in the concluding *Poco Allegro*. The imaginative touch of the *Poco Lento* link between the second movement and the Fugue demonstrates a characteristic sensitivity. It is a remarkably successful early work, often lyrical and expressive in the late-Romantic idiom of its day.

The Sonata acquires an historic importance if considered in the context of the history of British organ music of the present century. Gwilym Beechey, writing in 1968, regarded Parry's Toccata and Fugue in G 'The Wanderer' as 'the last important work of the 19th-century English Organ tradition; before it had been published and performed the Rhapsodies and Psalm-Preludes of Howells had made their appearance'. It can now be seen that Howells himself established the link between late Romanticism and early Modernism in his own Organ Sonata of 1911, and that this Sonata acquires the status accorded by Beechey to Parry's Toccata and Fugue.

At its publication eighty years after its composition the Organ Sonata in C Minor may now be assessed as a major discovery in British organ music of the twentieth century and in the output of Herbert Howells.

Graham Matthews, Robin Wells
July 1991

Duration: 26 minutes

This work is recorded on 'Parry and Howells: Organ Music' performed by Graham Matthews at the organ by N.P. Mander in Sheffield Cathedral, on the Herald Label: HAVPCD 116 (compact disc) and HAVPC 116 (cassette).

Front cover photograph, by Paul Coe, shows Howells in early 1918.

© Copyright 1992 Novello & Company Limited

All Rights Reserved

No part of this publication may be copied or reproduced in any form or by any means without the prior permission of Novello & Company Limited

Novello & Co. Ltd. welcomes information about performances of this work: details should be sent to the Performance Promotion Department at the above address.

SONATA No. 1

Edited by
Graham Matthews and Robin Wells

HERBERT HOWELLS
Op. 2

I

Allegro moderato e nobilmente

© Copyright 1992 Novello & Company Ltd.

All Rights Reserved

Sw.
mp
f
tr
sempre più tranquillo
p
pp
p
Solo clarinet
13
[Gt-Ped.off]
poco a poco
Sw.
pp
f
18
accel.
Gt
cresc.
ff
più sost.
marcato
23
[add Gt-Ped.]
poco allargando
ff
molto
27

See Preface for bars 45-6.

poco rit.
3
3
48
a tempo
Gt
pp
53
f
58
Sw.
pp
poco a poco accel.
ppp
Ch.
poco sf
pp
3
3
62
[add Ch.-Ped.]
[Ch.-Ped. off]

sempre poco a poco
ppp
pp
Gt
mf
67
[add Gt-Ped.]
accelerando
sempre più mosso - - - e forte
p
71
e cresc. - -
mf
75
Sw.
Gt
f
sempre cresc.
e stretto
79

più con fuoco ♩ = 120
ff
ff
ff
83
Più tranquillo ♩ = 100
mf
Sw.
87
Sw.
Gt
p
92
[Gt-Ped.off]
3
Sw.
marcato
96

7

ff
marcato molto
115
[Gt-Ped.off]
[Sw.]
mf
Ch.
pp
(Gt)
119
Ch.
pp
123
[Ch.]
pp
[add Gt-Ped.]
p
127

poco
Sw.
sost.
131
[Gt-Ped. off]
a
poco
più
[Sw.]
135
mosso
e
cresc
en
do
138
Gt
Gt
marcato
142
add Gt-Ped.
marcato

ff
146
150
ff
molto marcato
154
allargando
ff quasi Tromba
poco - - -
Sw.
fff pp molto legato
Sw.(full)
158
fff pp
[Gt- Ped. off]

a - - - - poco - - - - accel.
162
165
molto cresc.
allargando molto
ff
fff
168
fff [Gt-Ped.on]
Tempo primo
[Sw.]
ff
[Gt]
173
f
[Gt]
[Sw.]
f
[Gt]

[Sw.]
[Gt]
[Sw.]
più f
fff
177
[Gt]
ff dim.
181
Sw.
mp
f
tr
[sempre più tranquillo]
p
Ch.
[Sw.-Ch. off]
Ch. (Clarinet)
185
[Gt-Ped.off]
Sw.
pp
190

13

209
[add Ch.- Ped.]
poco tranquillo e meno
[mosso]
Ch.
Sw.
213
[Ch.- Ped.off]
poco rit.
217
a tempo
pp
Gt
p
pp
221

15

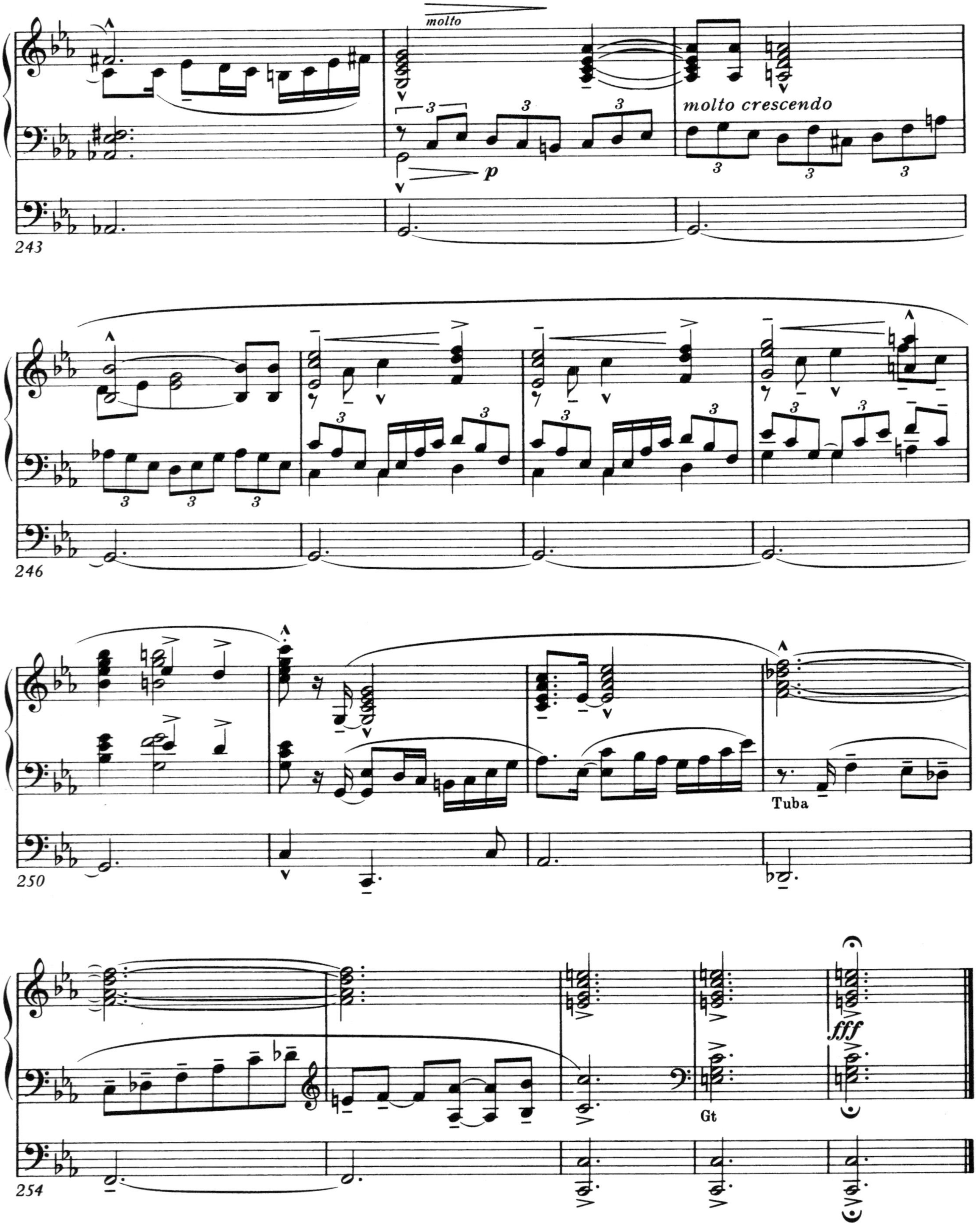
molto
p
molto crescendo
243
246
Tuba
250
Gt
fff
254

II

[Sw: *pp*
Gt: 8'
Ch: 8'
Sw.-Ped.]

Molto quieto, ma non troppo lento (♪ = 80)

10
Sw.
mp
f
p
Gt
p
dim.
13
pp
Sw.
più p
pp
[add Sw.-Gt]
16
Poco più lento (ma ♩ = ♪ of former time)
Sw.
pp e semplice
20

*The left hand stretches may be overcome by playing the suggested pedal [Ed.]

Più agitato; un poco più mosso
poco a poco accel.
pp
cresc.
pp
40
sempre accel. e più mosso
Gt
cresc.
43
add Gt-Ped.
f
mp
cresc.
46
f
f
49

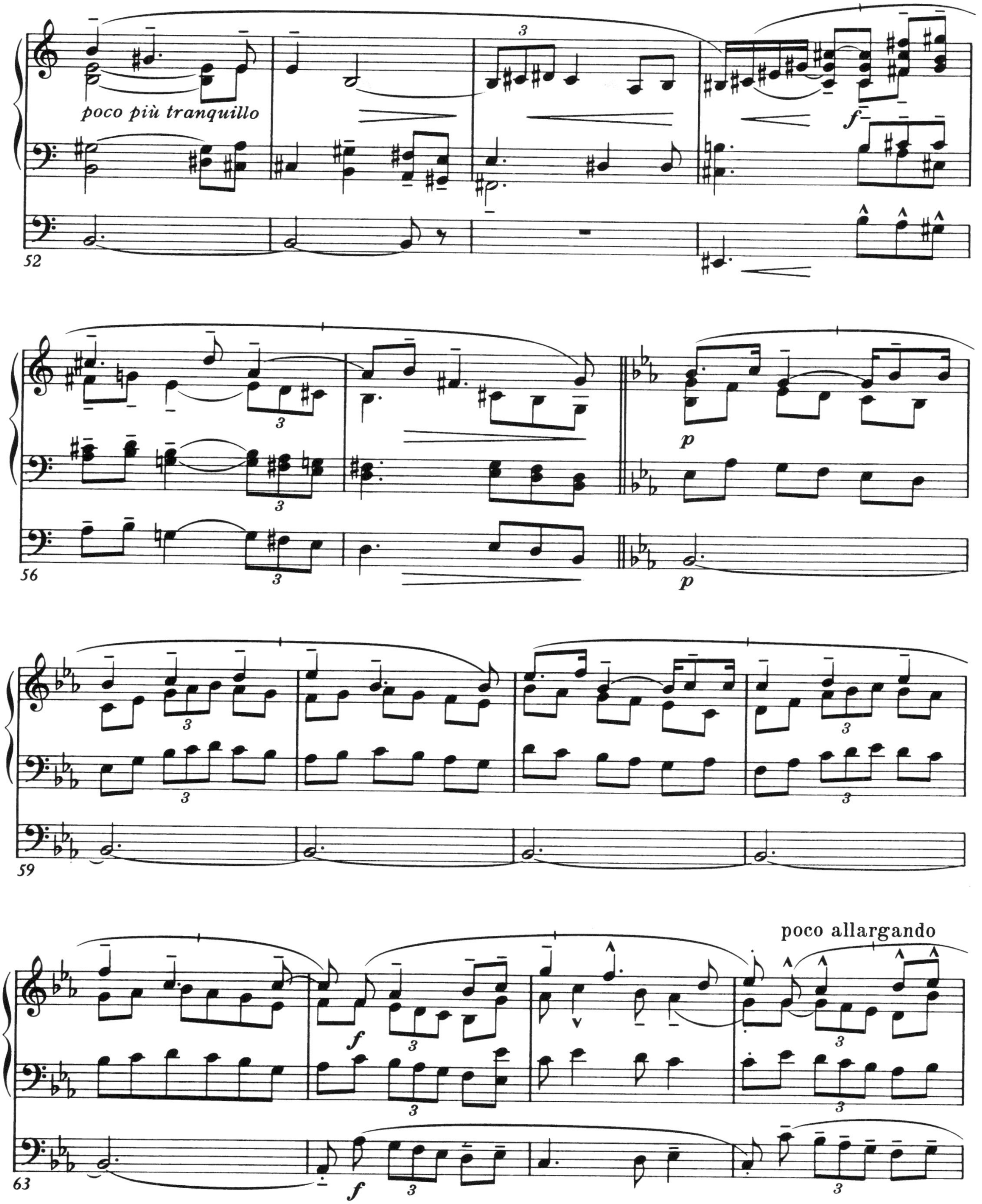
poco più tranquillo
52
56
59
63
poco allargando

molto meno mosso e maestoso
67
più rit. e dim.
p
Sw.
Sw.
71
[Gt-Ped. off]
Tempo primo
ppp e molto quieto
76
Ch.
pp
79

poco rit. e dim.
82
Sw.
ppp molto tranquillo
85
ritard.
88
mp
p
pp
ppp
91
attacca

III
Poco lento and Fugue

25

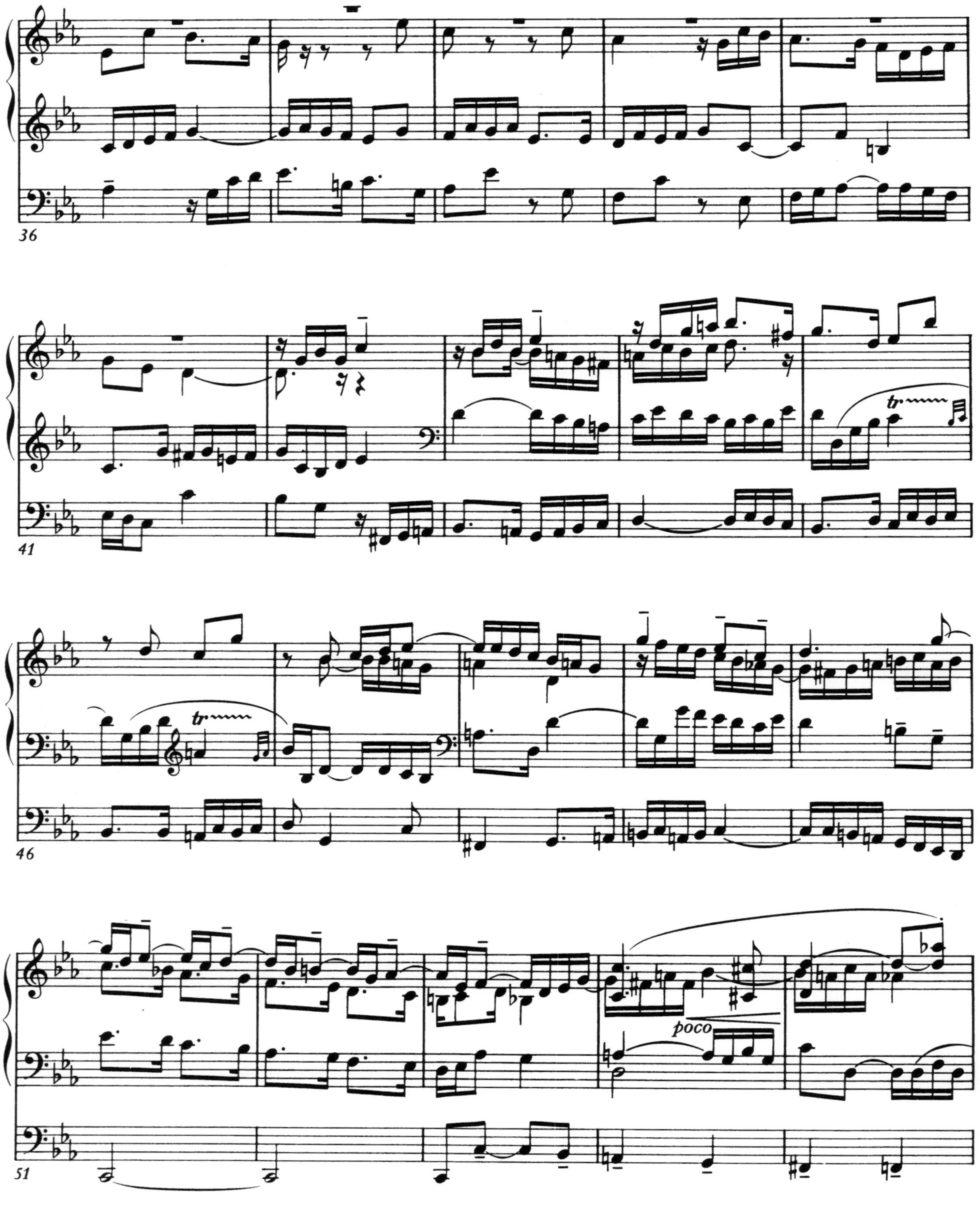
36
tr
41
tr
46
poco
51

27

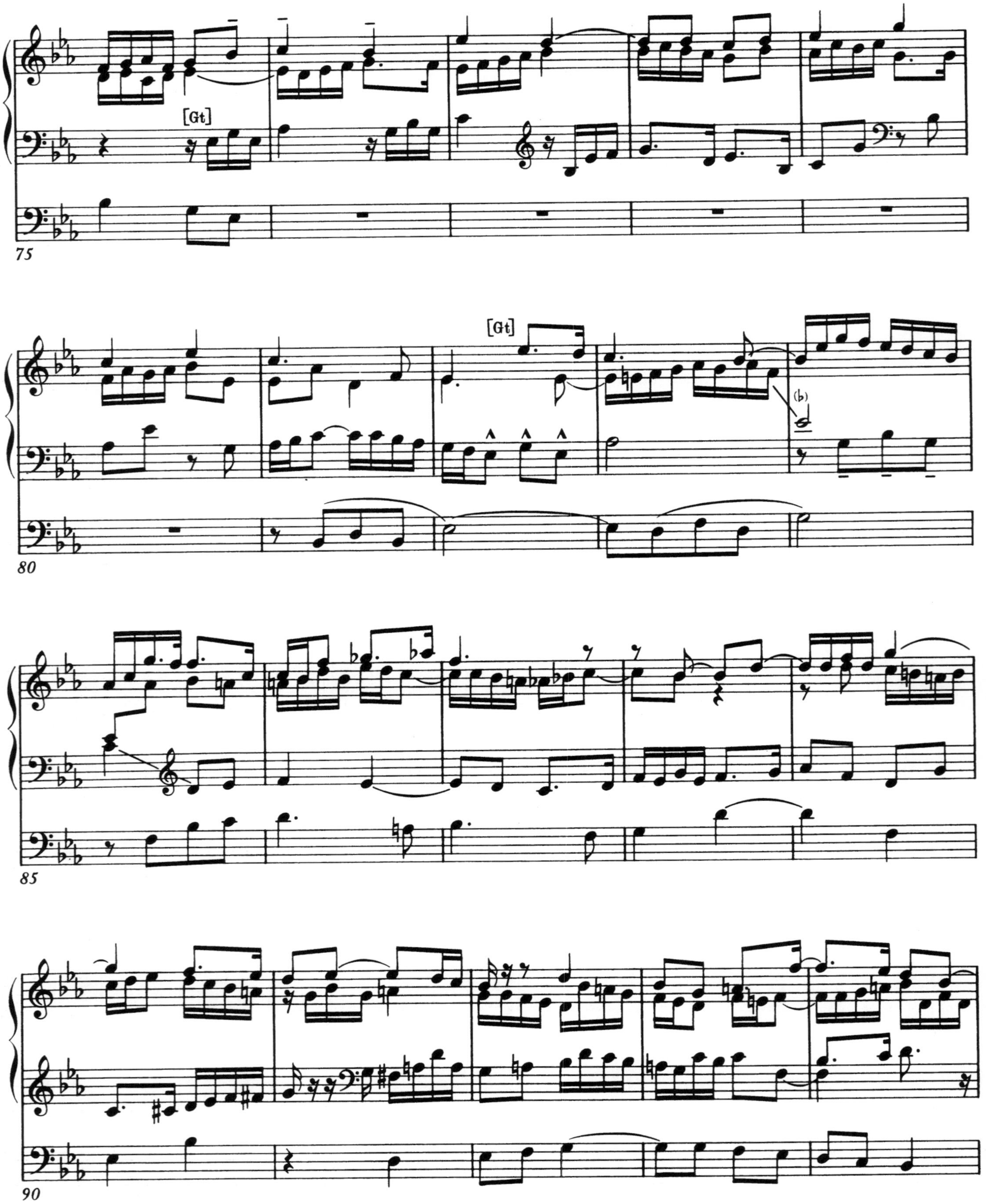
[Gt]
75
[Gt]
80
85
90

29

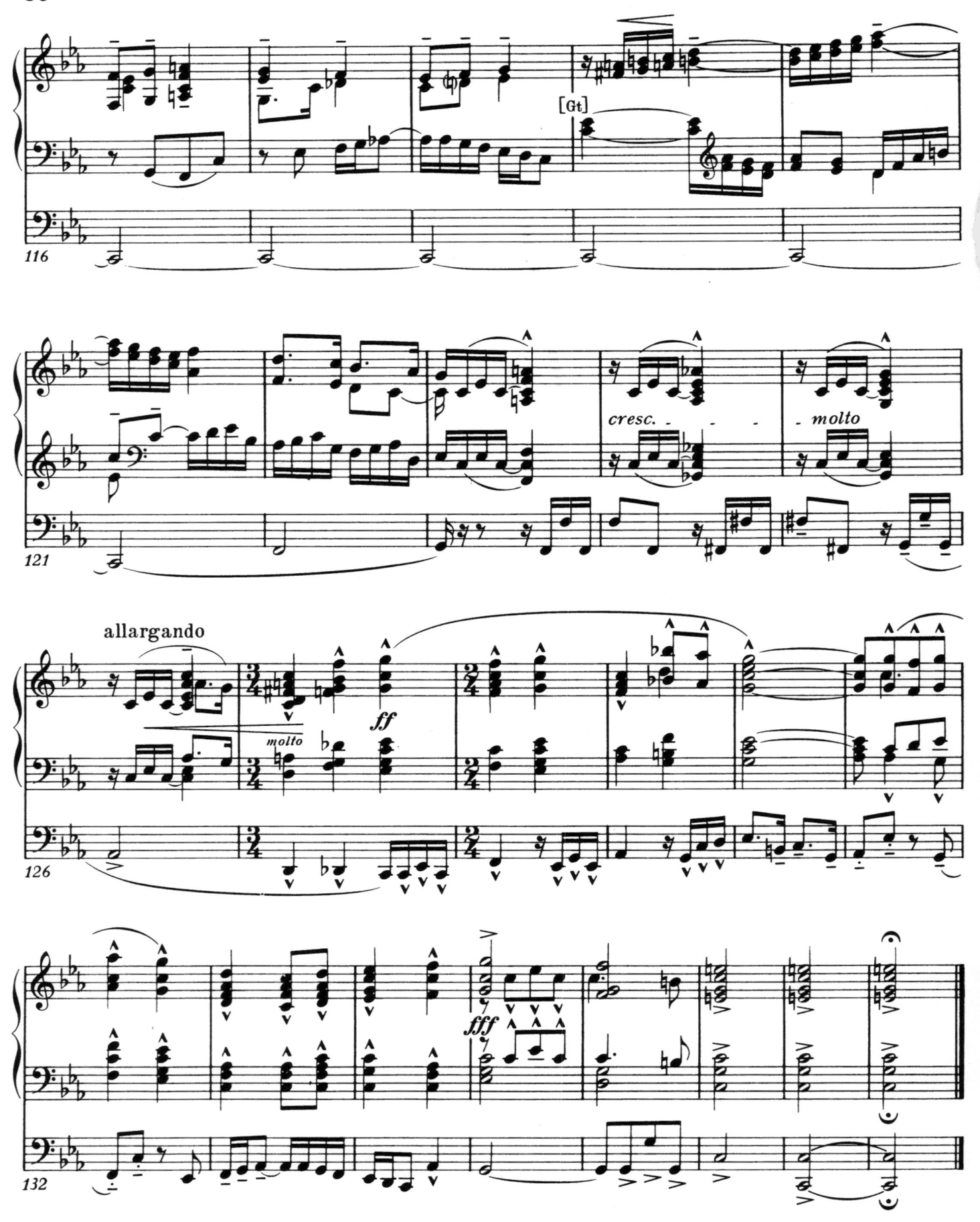

Printed in England